ALCTS Acquisitions Guides, No. 15

GUIDE TO VIDEO ACQUISITIONS IN LIBRARIES

Issues and Best Practices

MARY S. LASKOWSKI

Association for Library Collections
& Technical Services

AMERICAN LIBRARY ASSOCIATION
Chicago 2011

ALCTS ACQUISITIONS GUIDES

Writing RFPs for Acquisitions: A Guide to the Request for Proposal, #14
Frances C. Wilkinson and Linda K. Lewis, 84p. 2008, ALA.
ISBN: 978-0-8389-8483-3

Guide to Licensing and Acquiring Electronic Information, #13
Stephen Bosch et al., 112p. 2005, Scarecrow Press.
ISBN: 0-8108-5259-4

Guide to Out-of-Print Materials, #12
Narda Tafuri et al., 46p. 2004, Scarecrow Press.
ISBN: 0-8108-4132-0

Guide to Managing Approval Plans, #11
Susan Flood, 58p. 1998, ALA.
ISBN: 0-8389-3481-1

Guide to Performance Evaluation of Serials Vendors, #10
38p. 1997, ALA.
ISBN: 0-8389-3469-2

Guide to Selecting and Acquiring CD-ROMs, Software, and other Electronic Publications, #09
Stephen Bosch et al., 48p. 1994, ALA.
ISBN: 0-8389-0629-X

Guide to Preservation in Acquisition Processing, #08
Marsha J. Hamilton, 34p. 1993, ALA.
ISBN: 0-8389-0611-7

Guidelines for Handling Library Orders for Serials and Periodicals, 2d ed., #07
19p. 1992, ALA.
ISBN: 0-8389-3416-1

Statistics for Managing Library Acquisitions, #06
Eileen D. Hardy, 11p. 1989, ALA.
ISBN: 0-8389-3374-2

Guide to Performace Evaluation of Library Materials Vendors, #05
20p. 1988, ALA.
ISBN: 0-8389-3369-6

Guidelines for Handling Library Orders for In-Print Monographic Publications, 2d Ed, #04
Sara C. Heitshu, 21p. 1984, ALA.
ISBN: 0-8389-3148-0

Guidelines for Handling Library Orders for Microforms, #03
Harriet Rebuldela, 14p. 1977, ALA.
ISBN: 0-8389-3193-6

Guidelines for Handling Library Orders for Serials and Periodicals, #02
Murray S. Martin, 16p. 1974, ALA.
ISBN: 0-8389-3158-8

Guidelines for Handling Library Orders for In-Print Monographic Publications, #01
Murray S. Martin, 10p. 1973, ALA.
ISBN: 0-8389-3148-0

Association for Library Collections and Technical Services (ALCTS)
ALCTS is a division of the American Library Association

ALCTS Publishing
50 E Huron St
Chicago, IL 60611

www.ala.org/alcts

ISBN: 978-0-8389-8575-5

Library of Congress Cataloging-in-Publication Data
Laskowski, Mary S.
Guide to video acquisitions in libraries : issues and best practices / Mary S. Laskowski.
p. cm.
(ALCTS acquisitions guides ; no. 15)
ISBN 978-0-8389-8575-5
1. Acquisition of video recordings. 2. Acquisition of video recordings—United States. 3. Libraries—Special collections—Video recordings. I. Title.
Z692.V52L37 2011
025.2'873—dc22 2010053981

Published in the United States of America.

CONTENTS

PURPOSE AND SCOPE

This guide introduces video acquisitions to librarians who are new to the intricacies of video materials. Video material is defined as non-print audiovisual material such as feature films or documentaries in both analog and digital formats including VHS tapes, DVD discs, and streaming or downloadable digital files. The guide discusses issues and trends relating to video acquisitions and suggests basic best practices. References within the text and appendixes of selection and acquisition resources provide a broader review of the topic.

CHAPTER

1

VIDEO ACQUISITIONS

Anecdotal evidence suggests that many librarians suddenly find themselves responsible for video acquisitions without any background or experience to apply to the process. It is important to note that patron demand has driven the growth of many video collections, which is true for collections in academic, public, and school libraries. As stated in one article from the early 1990s, "Video has come of age.... It is to video collections that many libraries may now look for healthy circulation increases and to increased in patron demands for a wider range of library materials."[1] Increasing demand for robust video collections is one of the reasons that many librarians and other media professionals who may not have a background or requisite expertise in video selection and acquisition are assuming responsibility for video collections.

A fundamental underlying component necessary to success in video acquisitions is an understanding of why the collections exist and their importance within the overall library framework. The *Guidelines for Audiovisual and Multimedia Materials in Libraries and other Institutions*, created by the Audiovisual and Multimedia Section of the International Federation of Library Associations and Institutions (IFLA), offers a few general statements that are useful both for edifying new video librarians and for sharing with administrators and others who have an impact on funding, staffing, space allocation, and other necessary requirements for a thriving collection. As stated in the *Guidelines*,

> An ever-increasing amount of information—covering educational and recreational interests as well as information needs—is being produced in a

> wide range of audiovisual and electronic formats. Access to these materials should be as open and as free as access to print-based materials.[2]

While many educators and librarians are still reluctant to accord video collections the same prestige and attention that they do to print collections, the *Guidelines* provide some helpful counterpoints such as the fact that:

> audiovisual materials are part of our cultural heritage, carrying a huge amount of information that needs to be preserved for future use. The rich variety of media expressions in society should be reflected in the services offered to users by the libraries. . . . Audiovisual material can reach out to sections of the public for whom the traditional print-based materials have little impact, e.g., to those who are reluctant to use the printed work, and to those with visual and other handicaps. . . . In no circumstances should audiovisual materials be regarded as additional luxury materials but rather they should be considered as necessary components in a fully integrated library service.[3]

Although video materials should in no way be considered inferior to any other collection, it is important to recognize that video materials have presented a number of unique challenges in regards to library acquisitions, and will continue to do so for the foreseeable future. A good basic history of video in libraries, particularly in terms of video acquisitions, is *Video Acquisitions and Cataloging: A Handbook* by James C. Scholtz.[4]

THE UNIQUE NATURE OF VIDEO ACQUISITIONS

A number of basic differences between video formats and print materials, while perhaps obvious, have a significant impact on video collections and therefore video acquisitions. First, video acquisitions need to be viewed as temporary additions to the collection while print can often be considered permanent for most practical purposes. While many video formats, such as ¾" U-matic tapes, have a fairly long shelf-life, their accessibility is only as good as the availability of the playback equipment required to view them. It is an unfortunate fact that most video budgets do not reflect the need to replace or duplicate existing titles in new formats, and therefore there is a constant challenge to balance truly new acquisitions with the acquisition of duplicate titles in newer formats.

Second, unlike print formats, a wide variety of video formats are available at any given time. It is not enough to know the basic bibliographic information such as title, director, year of release, and actors because many titles are simultaneously or subsequently released in numerous formats. The patron or selector who suggested a purchase will not be best pleased if the title arrives in a format that is unusable for their particular situation. To complicate matters, it is not always clear to the patrons or selectors what formats are available for a particular title. Individuals who do not spend a lot of time working with video materials may not realize the differences between DVDs and Blu-ray discs, or between various region-coded DVDs, or that different equipment is required to view them. Therefore, it is vital for video librarians to not only understand the various formats available but also be able to explain them to others who may have no reason otherwise to have any knowledge in that area. It would often seem sufficient, for example, for a selector to indicate that they want a title that is available on VHS tape, without researching the availability of the VHS-NTSC format versus the VHS-PAL format. Educating the selectors about the variety of formats available to them, and what information is needed to place an informed order, is often the first step towards a smooth acquisitions process.

DIFFERING PHILOSOPHIES

Educating selectors about the ins and outs of video acquisitions is, of course, easiest if there are a small number of people who have responsibility for video selection. Unfortunately there are many different philosophies of shared responsibility for video collections, and in many of them there are multiple, even many, people who have input into collection development and the acquisitions process. Institutional models of video acquisitions structure vary by type of library and by institution.

The simplest model for video acquisitions, found across all types of libraries, is where there is one media librarian directly responsible for the video collection who oversees all aspects of the collection from purchase through circulation. In a more typical model, however, multiple selectors share responsibility for building and maintaining a video collection, and patron input is often highly utilized as well.

For example, in an academic library, subject bibliographers would select materials in all formats in their particular specialization and faculty and instructor requests in support of the curriculum provide some or even most of the direction for the collection. A survey conducted in spring 2003 indicated that roughly a third of video collections were managed by a media librarian who had sole responsibility for the video collection, while the remaining two-thirds followed a variety of models where responsibility for the video collection was spread among:

- acquisitions staff,
- subject bibliographers,
- media librarians in conjunction with acquisitions staff,
- media librarians with subject bibliographers,
- library managers,
- film studies departments, and
- faculty request only.[5]

Similar models exist in both the public and school library settings, but patron input varies widely from the general public to teachers or other educators to school or library boards.

One of the primary driving factors in determining what type of model is used is the collection development policy for the video collection, which usually depends on the assumptions made about the intended use of the collection. If the focus of the collection is to support research and instructional needs, the collection will tend to lean heavily towards educational documentaries and more unique content. A collection that is largely intended for personal recreational use will usually include more readily available mass-produced content. Obviously there is some overlap, as some larger collections will do both, and many times what is needed to support a particular curriculum will also prove to be of recreational value and vice-versa.

THE ACQUISITIONS PROCESS

As though the multitude of formats and selection processes were not complicated enough, the actual acquisition process for video materials often varies from that of traditional print. Susan McAdam states that video acquisitions is,

> an exciting part of any library. It's also the most volatile with the changing trends and the constantly updated technology. It takes an interested person with a true spark of exploration in his/her heart, someone anxious to communicate with colleagues and tenacious in the search for the most suitable materials. Anything less defeats the purpose.[6]

At some point along the line, either the selectors, or acquisitions folk if separate, need to have the necessary knowledge to effectively purchase video materials. A basic step-by-step overview of the acquisitions process can be found in James Scholz's handbook.[7]

Often, an entirely different strategy for acquisition of video must be employed, as a high percentage of desired titles may not be available through the same channels as the majority of print acquisitions. Many approval plans and jobber contracts do not include video materials and many video materials are only available through limited, sometimes unique sources. As Joanne Salce explains, "there are four main avenues towards acquiring video materials: wholesalers, distributors, catalog companies, and producers."[8] Salce clarifies the differences among the various avenues, defining a wholesaler as "a company that acquires a vast assortment of titles, selling them to a varied customer base," while a distributor can "not only acquire programming from independent producers, but also produce programming in-house, and can license programming, and sell it under its own name."[9] These fine distinctions become increasingly important when working with public performance rights or digital rights to content.

CHAPTER

2

PHYSICAL FORMATS

Understanding the wide variety of physical formats available at any given time and keeping track of formats on the horizon are key to effectively managing a video acquisitions process. Unlike a book, which regardless of size, language, binding, type of paper, or subject is still largely recognizable as a book and is generally accessible to anyone with any level of familiarity with print materials, video materials are only accessible by means of specific playback equipment, which may or may not be available for the duration of the life of the video itself. A good example is the ¾" U-Matic tape, which for many years was the industry standard for preservation of video content, and yet was never adopted as a popular solution in the home market, partially due to marketing and partially due to expense.

Currently, the home entertainment market drives the availability of various formats to an extensive degree. Obviously, acquisition of video materials needs to be in line with and informed by decisions regarding the adoption of specific physical formats. An excellent guide to the intricacies of the video collection development issues is Gary Handman's *Video Collection Development in Multi-type Libraries.*[10]

RAPIDLY CHANGING MARKETPLACE FOR NEW TECHNOLOGIES

A recent example of the rapidly changing marketplace for new technologies was the battle between the HD DVD and Blu-ray disc formats, both more advanced versions of DVDs with greater storage capacity but requiring different playback equipment. Toshiba, NEC, Sanyo, and Microsoft were a few of the companies that backed the development of the HD DVD, while others such as Panasonic, Pioneer, and Sony supported the Blu-ray disc. The winner at this point is clearly the Blu-ray disc, and yet the format is still similar enough to the standard DVD that many consumers avoided purchasing either, instead opting to wait it out and see if a standard was adopted before committing to a new technology. It is likely that the current mania for high-quality, high-definition everything will significantly impact the future home market.

The classic example of this of course was the format war between VHS and BetaMax videotape formats. Many large video collections still have Beta tapes (and surprisingly enough often Beta VCRs), demonstrating that even media professionals are prone to choosing poorly in the technological rivalry game. Though Sony BetaMax lost that battle in the 1970s and 1980s, Sony's announcement to support Blu-ray technology with the PlayStation3 helped edge out the HD DVD. As happened with the BetaMax format, early adopters may have chosen the HD DVD and now may be regretting that choice as the equipment becomes obsolete.

Most video collections at this point in time will consist primarily of both VHS tapes and DVDs. The percentage of each will be based on a variety of factors including how early the DVD format was accepted as a viable alternative to videotape, type of collection, and whether or not the decision was made to duplicate content in the newer DVD format or make a clean break from VHS to DVD wherever possible. As Sally Mason-Robinson stressed at a presentation in 1999, there are five major points to consider when deciding to add a new format such as DVD to a library collection:

1. Economy of scale. The library can only make this decision after a needs assessment and specific tracking of consumer trends.
2. Financial support of the institution, which includes budget approval for software and hardware and additional staff and their training, if needed.
3. Product sufficiency and quality.
4. Equipment. The product should be readily available and have sufficient tech support for library use.
5. The actual use that the product will have by the users.[11]

Given the complexity of factors to consider in the equation it should come as no surprise that each library adds new formats according to their own schedule. Recent developments indicate the VHS format has truly reached its end, and may soon officially be considered obsolete. One of last hold-outs for popular culture content on VHS, Distribution Video Audio Inc., shipped it's last VHS tape in December of 2008.[12]

PLAYBACK EQUIPMENT IN THE LIBRARY AND THE HOME MARKET

As with any new technological gadget or toy, new video formats take time to be adopted by a significant segment of the population. Significant, of course, often depends on the specific demographic a particular library serves. As stated in *Library Journal* in 2002,

> Librarians are listening to their patrons, which means libraries with different demographics may respond very differently. Libraries with large numbers of "early adopters"—often in suburban or high-tech areas—are, for example, moving into DVDs at a faster pace than libraries that serve rural or less affluent populations.[13]

In some cases the question is further complicated not only by ease of access to a particular type of viewing equipment but preferences for use. For example, when DVD drives were first becoming prevalent in laptops and desktop computers there was still a question as to whether or not viewing DVDs on a computer monitor was a viable alternative to standard playback equipment hooked up to a television. As an earlier study conducted by the author indicated, patrons who already had easy access to laptops still had concerns about sound quality and playback controls.[14] Though some percentage of the patron base for just about any library will include technophiles who want the latest, greatest, most expensive option available, each library needs to determine at what point there is a deep enough saturation of the market to make adding or switching to a new format a feasible option.

MARKETPLACE CONTROLS

It is important to remember that while libraries can and should impact the way the acquisitions process works and advocate for change with vendors and others, the market for video resources is big business and therefore market priorities are not often aligned with library needs. Particularly when dealing with mass-market materials such as feature films and popular television series, the focus is predominantly on protecting copyright and making as much money as possible from a product with little or no regard to library audiences. DVD region coding is one of the big challenges that has been introduced into the video acquisitions process. In order to better control pricing, release dates, and accessibility to content world-wide, motion picture studios created and successfully marketed the concept of different codes for different regions of the world that restrict playback of DVDs with that specific code to DVD players sold in that region. The list of region codes can be found in numerous places online. See figure 1.

Region Code	Geographical Regions
0, ALL or region free	Used for DVDs that are not encoded for a particular region but play in all
1	United States and Canada
2	Japan, Europe, South Africa, Middle East, Greenland
3	S. Korea, Taiwan, Hong Kong, Parts of South East Asia
4	Australia, New Zealand, Latin America (including Mexico)
5	Eastern Europe, Russia, India, Africa
6	Mainland China
7	Reserved for unspecified special use
8	Reserved for cruise ships, airlines, etc.

FIGURE 1: A very basic list of region codes.

Things get even more complicated when you take into consideration that a single DVD can have more than one code, and therefore play in a variety of regions, and that some geographical regions overlap multiple codes. The key to understanding region codes is that they correspond to particular hardware, and are not encryption codes per se. The frustration for libraries is that though most freeware and open source DVD players ignore region codes and will allow a user to view DVDs from any region, the commercial viewers and playback equipment are not so generous. Patrons may know how to adapt their own DVD drives to overlook region codes, but the legality of doing so is questionable at best, and usually negates any warranties on the hardware. For libraries, of course, the impact is potentially quite large, as materials purchased with region codes outside this country will not play on a standard U.S. DVD player. One solution is to buy region-free or multiregional DVD players, though there are legal questions there as well, particularly for players that do not recognize any region codes (the theory being that if the player recognizes the correct code and switches to that mode of play it is more legal than ignoring the coding completely). The difficulty of course is that while that may solve the problem within the confines of the library building, it does not help with classroom or home use of those materials. It also creates another technical aspect of the collection that may impact cataloging, marking, circulation policies, and create a far more complex problem than might normally be expected with the introduction of a new physical format.

The problem is similar to that of differentiating between NTSC, PAL and SECAM formats. A VHS tape is a VHS tape, right? Unfortunately no, as with DVDs, there are multiple formats with which a video acquisitions professional needs to be conversant. National Television Standards Committee (NTSC) is the format used predominantly in North America, Japan and Taiwan, while Phase Alternate Lines (PAL) is the format used mainly in Australia, New Zealand, United Kingdom and Europe. Sequential Color Memory (SECAM) was a French variation of PAL, used to improve signal transmission for PAL system televisions. Unlike region codes for DVDs, NTSC and PAL were standards mandated by the analog technology of televisions and the differing analog television signals that were sent and received in various parts of the world. The challenge for libraries was similar however, in that different players were required to view materials in the different standards.

As digital technology replaces analog throughout the world, the need for differing standards has diminished and will hopefully fade away completely. It was copyright protection and market value that drove the initial conception of region codes for DVDs, not technical differences. In some markets worldwide, such as Australia and New Zealand where restricted playback by region coding is not legal, region-free or multiregion players are the norm, and materials are coded for all regions. It is to be hoped that new formats will meet a more universal standard without introducing artificial barriers, but there is some evidence to the contrary in that Blu-ray DVDs are currently using a new system of region codes (A, B, and C), though some studios like Paramount Pictures and Universal Studios have released their titles without the region codes. Some Blu-ray players, much like some DVD players, are currently region free and backwards compatible with DVDs. Ideally licensing and copyright protection can be addressed in a way to satisfy the concerns of the producers and distributors of content without forcing technical barriers into the equation. While the theory is that the same title can be released in different regions on different schedules and with different pricing models, that fails to address those titles that may only be released in one region in the world but which are valued elsewhere and needed to build a particular curriculum or satisfy a particular need.

IMPACT OF CIRCULATION AND SUPPORT POLICIES

One of the biggest considerations in determining the appropriate point in time to add or switch to a new format is the intersection between collections acquired and circulation and support policies. If a particular collection circulates widely and the home market demands the acquisition of a new format, those would both be good indications that the time has come to add a new format. If, on the other hand, the home market does not yet widely support a format, or the library restricts access to the collection to building use, then the library would at a minimum need to support the equipment in-house to make the acquisition of a new format worthwhile. The reverse of course is also true, that if the home market no longer supports, or the library is unable to maintain playback equipment for a particular format, then the time has come to cease new acquisitions in that format and move on to those more widely accessible.

Though a broad circulation policy that allows multiple patron types to check materials out of the building argues in favor of supporting new formats as long as there is adequate saturation in the home market of appropriate playback equipment, open circulation policies also necessitate an investigation into the durability of various formats. There may be widespread adoption of a new format in the home market, but if the format is not durable enough to withstand multiple uses and at least occasional negligent care on the part of library patrons, then the library would need to either alter its circulation policies for specific formats (usually not a desirable proposition as it often results in chaos at point of circulation), build into the budget a high replacement percentage, or skip over that format in the hopes that the next format down the line will be more durable.

In addition to durability, collection security and preservation need to be considered in determining the appropriate intersection between circulation policies and acquisitions. In her article, Becky Albitz suggests that libraries must maintain a balance between preserving access to a collection in support of long-term research and curricular needs and meeting current demands for broad access to collections.[15] In her conclusion she states,

> In general, most effective media librarians proceed by balancing the security of the video collection against the service they hope to provide to the university community. If a policy is too restrictive, not only does the client go unserved, but the reputation of the library as an institution established to support instruction and research also suffers. If the policy is too lenient, the availability of the collection for research and instruction is also jeopardized. This balance may be difficult to achieve and maintain, but it can be done if the policy is flexible enough to accommodate adjustments when appropriate and the needs of the majority of clients continue to be met.[16]

Though the focus is clearly on academic institutions, the same principles hold true for public and school libraries. Both academic and school libraries often solve this puzzle by creating separate collections to serve different functions, such as a circulating collection of popular titles that circulate to students and a teaching or research collection of more expensive educational titles that circulate only to faculty or which may only be used in-house. Though this can be an effective solution, care needs to be taken that the collections and policies do not become so complex as to make managing them impractical. Such distinctions in policies and collections impact the acquisitions process, both in terms of educating all the appropriate selectors about what options and formats are available to them when purchasing for a specific collection, but also in knowing how the cataloging and technical services processes need to be handled upon receipt of the items in question.

Circulation policies also of course have a direct impact on the ability of libraries to preserve content for future use. Though there is always a temptation to limit use of collections to those who really need them in an effort to preserve them for later generations, the simple fact of most video collections is that due to changing formats and technologies, as well as the limited number of uses and difficulties in creating preservation copies, unless the video is intended for archives, video collections are living, evolving collections where individual items generally have relatively short life spans. To put it in a historical context familiar to most librarians, Ranganathan might as well have said: 1. Video is for use, 2. Every reader his [or her] video, and 3. Every video item its user.[17] Perhaps equally important would be two of the new laws recommended by Michael Gorman, to "2. Respect all forms by which knowledge is communicated, and 3. Use technology intelligently to enhance service."[18] Much as security of collections requires a balance, so does preservation for long-term use. The key element to creating a balanced policy is to identify the primary goals, patron base, and patron needs for the collection and build in replacement and reformatting as possible. Certainly it would be unfortunate to purchase an expensive educational documentary, loan it to all and sundry, and discover it scratched beyond repair when needed for the course for which it was recommended, but it would be equally unfortunate to house a wealth of video resources that are not accessible to most patrons and have them end up obsolete formats before getting used to their potential.

Other factors in the decision-making process regarding new physical formats are the support policies in place at the institution. Though this is of particular concern in the academic and school settings, it comes into play in public libraries as well. In the academic environment this usually comes down to what playback equipment is supported in classrooms, and therefore what formats are readily accessible to faculty for classroom use. Often the equipment supported in the classrooms is installed and maintained by a different department than the library, and therefore requires a collaborative partnership with other campus units to facilitate ease of use and accessibility of purchased materials. The same principle carries over to the school library, where teachers need to be able to use materials in some or all classrooms in order to use them to their greatest potential as teaching tools. Though in many cases the collaborative arrangements in a school setting will require fewer participants, it is also the case that many video collections are shared across units or districts and need to be accessible to the broadest possible number of teachers.

The public library setting differs a bit, in that the focus may be on home use, but there are also considerations of support for playback equipment in venues for public viewings, either in the library or other public buildings. Updating the playback equipment across multiple viewing spaces, be they classrooms or other venues, is a pricey proposition, and often is a factor in continuing to purchase a slightly outdated format if that is what is readily supported.

CHAPTER

3

PRODUCTION AND VENDOR ISSUES

Making the decision about what formats to acquire based on the playback equipment available is, of course, only the first step in the battle. Sufficient content must be available to make acquisition a viable prospect. Availability in this context means not only content that is produced, but content that is accessible to libraries through appropriate acquisitions channels. The challenges are that

> vendor selection is perhaps the most challenging component of video acquisitions. For feature films, the difficulty lies in finding a single vendor able to handle most orders without substantial intervention from the library staff. The ideal is a vendor able to process video orders in much the same way as book orders. For documentaries, the difficult task is identifying the distributor best able to supply each individual title.[19]

PREVALENCE OF THE SMALL INDEPENDENTS

Many libraries, particularly public libraries, school libraries, and those of smaller institutions, rely almost exclusively on approval plans or aggregate jobbers to gain the widest assortment of materials from the fewest possible sources. This not only simplifies the acquisitions process and record keeping, but can help with selection and processing of materials once received. While this is a perfectly viable solution for many materials, it does not, unfortunately, work well for video, especially for larger collections or those that specialize in unique content. Many independent filmmakers either end up distributing their films themselves or working with other small distributors to market their content. It is fairly rare for an independent documentary, for example, to be picked up and distributed in a fashion that would allow libraries to purchase through their usual book vendors.

In order to acquire any of these unique titles the library needs to set up many individuals or small companies as vendors, often for quite limited purchases. Obviously this has an impact on both the speed of the order process as well as the investment in staff time.

ADHERING TO APPROVAL PLANS OR CONTRACTS

Another possible complication in streamlining the acquisition of video materials is possible contract or licensing issues with existing approval plan vendors or jobbers. Though contracts often significantly increase the discounts given to the institution, care must be taken that the license or contract terms of the service do not preclude the institution from entering into additional, simultaneous plans with other vendors for content that is not readily available from a single source. Ideally, the library is able to work with multiple vendor plans to provide access to a wide variety of content without resorting solely to one-off firm orders for specific content on a title-by-title basis.

ADOPTION RATES OF NEW FORMATS AND TECHNOLOGIES

Though saturation of the home market and availability of playback equipment at the institution are key factors in making the decision to start collecting in a new format, the unfortunate truth is that even once a decision has been made it is often difficult to acquire specific or unique content in a particular format. Though the home market is a good indicator of the availability of mass-produced content such as feature films and popular television series, there is no guarantee that the educational market will follow quickly or at all before there is yet another new development in available video formats. Using the VHS to DVD migration as an example, the availability of educational content in DVD format lagged behind the home market significantly.

The problem is multifaceted. To begin with, distributors of independent documentaries for example may not have the appropriate infrastructure to readily adapt to production of a new format. They may also be leery of choosing poorly, and therefore rely on a massive adoption of the new format at the institutional level to drive up demand before committing to producing content using new technology. In some cases the vendor may not have the rights to distribute the content in anything but the original format, and sadly, in many cases, the content is never redistributed in newer formats at all. This leads to a significant problem with legacy collections where the content is not available in any new video format and yet the original playback equipment may not be considered officially obsolete, which would allow for some consideration under copyright law to reformat as needed. Even should reformatting be legally possible, the cost investment at the institutional level is prohibitive.

Pricing Schemes: Educational *vs.* Home Market

In addition to possible delays in availability in newer formats, there are significant differences in pricing models between educational vendors and the home market. Many selectors are horrified to discover that, unlike the $17 newly released popular feature film that they just purchased for their home, the documentary they would like to add to the collection costs $290 in the same format. It is not at all unusual for educational materials to run ten times the cost of mass-produced popular content, and the educational materials may not come with any additional rights. In other words, the extra hundred or more dollars spent per educational title may not equate to any added benefit in terms of public performance or other use rights, and instead is simply the cost of acquiring that specialized content with the same limited rights as any other commercially produced title.

There are myriad reasons why the pricing models differ so greatly between the educational and home markets. The most compelling seems to be that mass-produced popular content is intended for sale to an extremely large audience, allowing the price to be low while still making a large profit. Much educational content is produced by independents or small distributors who sell to a much smaller market of schools and libraries and therefore need to price their content higher in order to recoup the cost of production. While not always the case, it is also true that the educational content may come with public performance rights allowing the library or institution to use the material for public screenings, which is pretty much never the case with mass-produced popular content.

An issue to be aware of is that sometimes the same educational content is available from different vendors at widely varying prices and license terms, and in some cases available from the same vendor with a structured pricing model that differs by type of library or use. For example, a historical biography might be distributed by one vendor for the home market, and by another to libraries. The home-market version may or may not differ slightly in terms of extras and the educational version in most cases would include some form of public performance rights. What is often truly frustrating is when the same distributor has a tiered pricing model that attempts to limit libraries to purchasing the content at a higher price, while offering a lower price to individuals. Again, the library price may include additional rights, but in some cases those rights are not needed. If the library needs the content solely for face-to-face classroom use and does not intend to use for any public screenings there may be no need to invest in a copy that comes with public performance rights, though the vendor may not allow the library to purchase at the home-market price. Knowing the needs of the library and investigating available options can often lead to significant cost savings.

Serial Replacement Issues

Much as serial publications in print present special challenges during and after acquisition, many video materials pose similar problems. Though most video materials are not truly serial in nature, meaning that in almost all cases specific firm orders must be placed for desired content rather than open-ended serial subscriptions, some of the issues remain the same. For example, though individual orders for each season of a television series may need to be placed as they are released in a given format, it is often very difficult to purchase or replace an individual episode or disc from within a larger set. This makes it costly to provide access for what may be a limited need, or to actively replace missing or damaged materials without paying for an entire set. This problem is perhaps most prevalent with television series, especially given their mass-produced nature, but also occurs for sets of educational materials. In some cases, if a volume of an educational set needs to be replaced the vendor could work with the library to replace the volume at an individual price or might replace the set at a reduced price, so it is always worth while to contact the vendor directly and alert them to the need and discuss options. For mass-produced content however, there is usually little option other than to purchase an entire replacement set or series or do without. Very few vendors, such as Midwest Tape, market individual replacement discs for series replacement.[20]

Copy Quality Differences

A less frequent, but potentially more difficult, problem is that on occasion the same title will be available from different vendors at the same time, or subsequently, but the quality of the print widely differs. A distributor may acquire the rights to sell a particular title, but either not have access to a high-quality master to work from, or have a lower-quality production run that other distributors. Many media professionals find themselves in the awkward position of attempting to explain that the library copy of a title was in fact legally purchased, when the quality of the copy appears to be that of a homemade copy or something taped from television. Or, in some instances explaining that though a patron or instructor may own a high-quality copy in their personal collection, the commercially available copy owned by the library is not actually defective or damaged but simply from a different production run. If ordering materials from a vendor who is previously unknown, or who may not always deliver the highest-quality product, it is always advisable to actually view the item before irrevocably adding to the collection, or requesting a preview copy before purchase if possible.

Out-of-Print Video

Another difficulty in acquiring video materials is the accelerated rate at which they often go out of print. It is not unlikely to wait months or longer for a much-needed title to become available, or available in a new format, only to discover that after the first production run it is completely unavailable for purchase again. As Gary Handman notes that the seemingly ubiquitous nature of video can

> provide a false and frustrating illusion of easy, endless access to a robust, ever-expanding universe of materials . . . . Doubly unfortunate is the fact that for many categories of video, materials that have fallen out of the catalogs or off the trade lists do so forever, and are nearly impossible to acquire after the fall.[21]

Unlike the book industry, there are not a lot of dependable options for acquiring out of print video titles. Alibris is one of the few out-of-print traditional library vendors who carries out-of-print video, and the selection is somewhat limited.[22] Many titles, of course, are available through sources such as Amazon, third-party vendors, or eBay, but often require credit cards to purchase (sometimes problematic for library acquisitions departments, particularly if the price is under a certain limit), and there is no guarantee regarding the quality or viability of the copy. It can be extremely difficult to determine if a copy purchased from a third party is a pirated copy or truly a used but legally produced copy. Additional tips and sources can be found in the report of the ALCTS Out-of-Print Discussion Group report from 2002.[23]

CHAPTER

4

LICENSING AND COPYRIGHT ISSUES

One of the most complicated challenges facing media librarians is understanding the various licensing and copyright issues that impact the use of video in the classroom and public venues. Though some of these copyright issues do not specifically relate to the acquisitions process, a basic understanding of the principles involved is required to make informed decisions regarding acquisitions policies. The pertinent copyright laws can be found on the Library of Congress Copyright Office web site (http://www.copyright.gov/). Another excellent resource for further interpretation of copyright law and patron education is the Stanford Copyright & Fair Use site (http://fairuse.stanford.edu/).

PUBLIC PERFORMANCE RIGHTS

Perhaps the biggest controversy regarding licenses and copyright as related to video acquisitions is the question of public performance rights. Many educational video resources are sold with public performance rights (PPR), sometimes as a higher-priced option and sometimes included in the basic purchase price. Feature films and other popular content such as television shows, however, are not available with public performance rights, and therefore public performance rights need to be licensed as required. The controversy arises from what constitutes a public performance, and whether or not institutions are required to obtain public performance rights to fill their basic needs. In simplest terms, a public performance is usually defined as any screening of video content that is open to the public (as opposed to students enrolled in a course). Understanding the needs of the patrons using the video collection is key to video acquisition in this area, as much funding can be lost unnecessarily by purchasing public performance rights if not necessary. Non-profit educational institutions make use of the face-to-face teaching exemption for classroom use of video, and many public and other libraries do not have robust public screening programs, so the question really becomes the primary purpose of the collection and whether or not the library considers public performance rights part of its mission to the community served.

The face-to-face teaching exemption is found in section 110 of title 17 of copyright law:

> Notwithstanding the provisions of section 106, the following are not infringements of copyright:
>
> > (1) performance or display of a work by instructors or pupils in the course of face-to-face teaching activities of a nonprofit educational institution, in a classroom or similar place devoted to instruction, unless, in the case of a motion picture or other audiovisual work, the performance, or the display of individual images, is given by means of a copy that was not lawfully made under this title, and that the person responsible for the performance knew or had reason to believe was not lawfully made.[24]

The Technology, Education, and Copyright Harmonization (TEACH) Act of 2002 amended section 110 by substituting new language for paragraph 110(2), expanding the exemption to include transmission of content for distance education provided additional stipulations regarding technological security and copyright education are met. Therefore, if the primary focus of the collection is to serve the classroom use or personal research needs of instructors, and other use is limited to personal circulation transactions not intended for public performance, there may be no need for the library to invest in public performance rights, though in some cases there is no option available but to do so. When public performance rights are required, for libraries engaged in public film screenings for example, often a temporary public performance license can be acquired through a third party such as Swank Motion Pictures, Inc.[25]

REFORMATTING OPTIONS

An advantage (if it can be called that) to video formats becoming outdated at such an alarming rate is that copyright law makes specific exceptions for reformatting obsolete formats. While reformatting options may not specifically relate to video acquisitions, part of the process requires an excellent understanding of what is currently available to purchase, both generally in terms of knowing what formats are considered obsolete, and more specifically whether or not individual titles have been rereleased in newer formats, thus making them ineligible for reformatting locally. That being the case, it is often part of the role of the video acquisitions specialist to help determine the legality of specific reformatting requests. The pertinent information is found in section 108 of copyright law:

> (a) Except as otherwise provided in this title and notwithstanding the provisions of section 106, it is not an infringement of copyright for a library or archives, or any of its employees acting within the scope of their employment, to reproduce no more than one copy or phonorecord of a work, except as provided in subsections (b) and (c), or to distribute such copy or phonorecord, under the conditions specified by this section, if—
>
>> (1) the reproduction or distribution is made without any purpose of direct or indirect commercial advantage;
>>
>> (2) the collections of the library or archives are (i) open to the public, or (ii) available not only to researchers affiliated with the library or archives or with the institution of which it is a part, but also to other persons doing research in a specialized field; and
>>
>> (3) the reproduction or distribution of the work includes a notice of copyright that appears on the copy or phonorecord that is reproduced under the provisions of this section, or includes a legend stating that the work may be protected by copyright if no such notice can be found on the copy or phonorecord that is reproduced under the provisions of this section.[26]

Additional information found in section 108 indicates that a digital copy may not be distributed beyond the premises of the library or archive, that a reasonably priced copy cannot be commercially available in order for the library to avail themselves of this exemption, and that a format is considered obsolete if "the machine or device necessary to render perceptible a work stored in that format is no longer manufactured or is no longer reasonably available in the commercial marketplace." One of the difficulties in the way the law is worded is that an exemption is made possible if the legally acquired library-owned copy has been damaged or stolen, but of course if that is the case there is no copy readily available to duplicate and the library must rely on other copies existing at other institutions to derive a replacement.

LICENSING FOR DISTRIBUTING DIGITAL VIDEO

One key factor sometimes forgotten in interpreting copyright exemptions is that if the library has signed a contract that specifically precludes certain types of use of the resource, that license in effect trumps any exemption that might otherwise have made the resource broadly accessible. Of particular concern when dealing with the licensing of digital video for streaming or downloading is language that may limit the right of the institution and its authorized community to excerpt material from the source. An excellent place to gain a basic understanding of licensing concepts and terms and to find examples of contract language that may or may not be acceptable depending on various institutional needs is the Liblicense web site hosted by Yale (http://www.library.yale.edu/~llicense/intro.shtml). There is no industry standard for licensing digital video and many factors such as obtaining digital rights and tracking rights holders, identifying and meeting various institutional needs, and pricing models vary widely among vendors.

FAIR USE AND COPYRIGHT LAW

Libraries make use of fair use across all formats and in numerous different situations and fair use plays an important role in video services. The fair use copyright exemption states that:

> Notwithstanding the provisions of sections 106 and 106A, the fair use of a copyrighted work, including such use by reproduction in copies or phonorecords or by any other means specified by that section, for purposes such as criticism, comment, news reporting, teaching (including multiple copies for classroom use), scholarship, or research, is not an infringement of

> copyright. In determining whether the use made of a work in any particular case is a fair use the factors to be considered shall include—
>
> (1) the purpose and character of the use, including whether such use is of a commercial nature or is for nonprofit educational purposes;
>
> (2) the nature of the copyrighted work;
>
> (3) the amount and substantiality of the portion used in relation to the copyrighted work as a whole; and
>
> (4) the effect of the use upon the potential market for or value of the copyrighted work.
>
> The fact that a work is unpublished shall not itself bar a finding of fair use if such finding is made upon consideration of all the above factors.[27]

In addition to the fair use copyright exemption, there have been other guidelines developed specifically for the use of video. One such example is the Kastenmeier guidelines, which provide best practices for the retention and use of video resources taped off the air.[28] Much as the intended use of video resources can impact the necessary license pursued or purchase of public performance rights, the interpretation and application of copyright law and exemptions can impact acquisitions processes and decisions. For example, the Kastenmeier guidelines preclude the use of content taped off the air after forty-five calendar days, leading many educators to request expedited purchase of the same content and necessitating an understanding of the cycle from on-air programming to commercial availability. Additional resources for understanding best practices in the use of video resources in educational settings are:

- The Code of Best Practices in Fair Use for Video Literacy Education (http://www.centerforsocialmedia.org/resources/publications/code_for_media_literacy_education/)
- The Society for Cinema and Media Studies' Statement of Best Practices for Fair Use in Teaching for Film and Media Educators (http://www.cmstudies.org/documents/SCMSBestPracticesforFairUseinTeaching-Final.pdf).

CHAPTER

5

STREAMING AND DOWNLOADABLE VIDEO

For years there has been a growing sentiment, particularly on the part of those who may not be intimately involved in video librarianship, that soon all the problems inherent in collecting various physical formats for video content will go away because everything will be available online. Unfortunately, though there is certainly the potential for video content to be heavily used online, and by being online take advantage of all the possible benefits such as broader accessibility (24/7 access from anywhere over the Internet), the inherent problems currently weigh at least as heavily as the potential benefits. Any savings in efficiency of physical space, circulation staff, physical preparation such as marking, and the elimination of the need to support physical formats with specific playback equipment is countered by the increased complexity of licensing, lack of consistent availability, file preservation and migration issues, often prohibitive pricing models and technical support, not to mention the aesthetic quality of the experience. However, as one author comments,

> If "why" libraries should make digital video available is obvious, the "how" is not. There is no one answer to the question of how to build or support digital video collections. Institutions that wait for that technological solution will wait for a long, long time, missing opportunities to provide valuable resources to their user communities.[29]

LIMITED NUMBER OF VENDORS

As with any new physical format, there has to be sufficient buy-in and support from vendors and distributors to make the new format a feasible proposition for libraries, and digital video is no exception. And, contrary to commonly held belief, digital video does not simplify the complexities of dealing with multiple physical formats, as there is no file format adopted as an industry standard. Different libraries have widely varying needs for digital formats, and producers have great difficulty predicting the needs of the market. Another major stumbling block from the distributor's standpoint is that they may not own all of the necessary rights to then sell digital rights with or instead of the physical copy. The lack of a widely adopted standard, combined with the complexity of managing digital rights, has led many distributors to be slow to offer digital rights for their titles which, much like when dealing with physical formats, has significantly slowed the adoption rate on the part of libraries pending ready availability of sufficient content to make the transition worthwhile. However, it should be noted that for many institutions the need for licensed digital content to be used for distance education continues to push the market in this direction in spite of ongoing problems and concerns. It is increasingly important for librarians to communicate concerns and expectations regarding the availability of appropriate licensing and pricing schemes to the industry at large. This is a concern shared by many librarians who deal with licensing of any form of electronic resources:

> In the digital era librarians simply have to be more demanding and expect more from our vendors. The very important role that is emerging for our librarians is a redefinition of their role as information mediators. To make this role even more important, librarians need to add value to the information as it moves through this chain. The added value does not come from passively relaying the information we receive from the producers on to the consumers. The added value comes from insisting on quality products at reasonable prices.[30]

MASS-MARKET TITLES *VS.* EDUCATIONAL TITLES

Much as there are major cost and availability differences between mass-market commercial titles and educational titles for video in physical formats, there are vast differences when considering digital video between the two very different markets. As with the introduction of region codes for DVDs, the creators of mass-market titles are not particularly concerned with the needs of libraries or their patrons and are focused exclusively on making a profit through the largest amount of sales. That being the case, there are major concerns from feature film producers regarding pirating and other issues that might adversely affect the marketplace that make them extremely hesitant if not outright unwilling to consider distribution of digital rights to content. With few exceptions the only feature film content available to libraries with digital rights are part of large package services such as Overdrive, as most feature film content and television series that are available online have individual license restrictions that specifically preclude library distribution to multiple patrons.[31]

On the other hand, many educational producers, vendors and distributors are quite willing to work with libraries to provide digital rights to educational titles for institutional use, but the process is time-consuming on both ends. Partly due to the lack of an industry standard, and partly due to the widely varying needs of each institution and corresponding options for licensing, it often takes months to pursue the rights to an individual title. If there is a time-sensitive request or need for specific content, it is practically impossible in the current environment to pursue digital rights unless there is already a pre-existing contract or service in place to provide digital access through that particular vendor. For example, if an instructor at an educational institution wants the library to purchase a specific video title for use with a particular class or to place on reserve for an upcoming semester, it is highly unlikely that a new contract can be negotiated to accommodate that need in a timely enough fashion, while a physical copy of the video format can be rush ordered and available in a few days. The fact that providing access to the content online requires licensing, while providing the physical copy for circulation does not, severely limits the feasibility of pursuing digital rights to fill certain needs. On the other hand, as with the print environment, once the licensing is complete to allow access online, the much broader accessibility is a major benefit to the community served.

COMPATIBILITY ISSUES AND PROPRIETARY FORMATS

Though the situation has improved somewhat in recent years, there is an ongoing debate regarding appropriate file formats for digital video, and of course ongoing competition between various proprietary file formats and platforms. There is also great debate regarding preservation of digital files, similar to that which is occurring regarding serials, but not nearly as far advanced yet in terms of delineating the responsibilities of the producer or vendor versus those of the institution, acceptable file formats, and others.

The clearest example of file format issues to articulate is that of the end-users viewing options. Much as physical formats require specific playback equipment, different file formats require different video players to be used. Or perhaps more importantly, different video players often require different file formats. There are a number of big names in the video player world, perhaps most notably RealPlayer, Windows Media Player, QuickTime, Apple iTunes, and Adobe Flash. Most video players play a variety of file types in addition to their own proprietary file formats, and have slightly different interfaces and options available. From the end-user standpoint, the players themselves can be downloaded for free, so the frustration comes from having to make sure that you have the most recent version of the software and possibly having to have more than one player loaded on a computer in order to access various file types. The institutional perspective is much more complicated, as though the player may be free, the hardware and software to develop and support the appropriate digital files are not. Maintaining multiple duplicative file formats for the same content is costly, as is the necessary hardware, such as appropriate proprietary servers. Issues to consider when deciding on a digital video file format include image quality, cost of proprietary hardware and software for storage, and the possible existing dependency of various constituents on existing file formats. It is possible that recent trends towards incorporating executable video files directly into web pages using Flash Video will help alleviate some of these problems, but there is by no means a consensus regarding the best way to provide stable, reliable access to digital video files with the highest quality possible. The debate will likely continue until there is a high-quality industry standard that is readily accessible to the lowest common denominator in terms of required technological infrastructure. Clearly, the format issues are no less complex in the digital realm than for physical formats.

PRICING SCHEMES

Once a library has determined what file formats can be supported and has the technical infrastructure in place to support content, content must then be licensed to suit the needs of patrons. Just as there were similarities between types of physical video formats and either print monographs or print serials, there are similarities between the acquisition of digital video files and e-books and e-journals. As mentioned already, many of the benefits are obvious, such as access at any time of day and from remote locations. Unfortunately, many of the similarities to other types of e-content relate to the complexity of the licensing and the necessary time and resource investment in making the materials accessible in a timely fashion. Just as there is not a universal file format for digital video, there is no standard contract for licensing the content once the file format has been determined. Ideally, an institution would be able to identify the type of license desired and be able to pursue that model across different vendors to secure content in multiple subject areas in a uniform fashion. In reality, each vendor has different criteria for licensing, and different pricing models to match. For example, in some cases licensing the digital rights to content requires purchasing a full-price copy of the existing physical format and then doubling or tripling the cost to add in digital rights. In some cases, the physical format and digital rights are sold separately, even occasionally from different vendors. Given that much of the availability of digital rights depends on complicated rights management done by vendors with varying degrees of success and availability, there is no particular rhyme or reason to how digital rights are priced except to expect the unexpected.

CONVERTING PHYSICAL FORMATS TO DIGITAL FILES

One of the factors that can dramatically affect the pricing structure for digital rights is whether or not the digital files are produced by a vendor or if the library can or must create the digital files locally from the physical format. If a library has the technical infrastructure in place to support file conversion, it can save quite a bit of money up front, though of course the cost is then distributed elsewhere in the library. In some cases an institutional inability to locally create the appropriate digital files precludes the licensing of certain content, as some vendors and producers also lack the ability to create the appropriate derivative files and require the institution to do so. There are several advantages to converting the physical format to digital file locally at the institution. Most notably, assuming that the license allows, is the ability to reformat as needed if the institutional model for access changes to a different file type, or if there is a need to remaster if the file gets corrupted. Also, if an institution is just beginning to figure out a plan for streaming files, the ability to create the files locally can provide a great deal of feedback about what is feasible, what works best in that environment, what patrons like or do not like, etc. The drawbacks include the necessary investment in a technological infrastructure, the possible time delays depending on the availability of staffing and resources, and the possible lack of appropriate expertise in this area if not done on a routine basis.

PURCHASE *VS.* LEASING: NEEDS OF DIFFERENT LIBRARIES

Part of the difficulty vendors and distributors of video content encounter with the need for procuring digital rights is that not only do the rights holders to the content have differing ideas about what they are willing to license and what they need to retain, but different types of institutions, and even each individual institution within a type, has widely varying needs. Larger academic institutions with larger video budgets and excellent technology support may prefer to purchase unlimited digital rights to content in perpetuity, believing that such licensing is the only way to guarantee long-term access in a way that is comparable to the rest of the research/teaching collection. Smaller academic institutions, or institutions such as public and school libraries, which do not have the same research collection mandates, may prefer to license popular content for a limited time, knowing that once the license expires there will be newer, more sought after content available.

Though part of the equation remains the availability of appropriate technical support, the differing philosophies play a major role in the need for flexibility in licensing options to suit different needs. Academic institutions and patrons are, in a rather unfortunate way, already accustomed to the need to use a variety of different platforms and user interfaces to search for available content and information housed in numerous catalogs and databases. While every effort may be made to simplify the process for patrons, and provide a one-stop shopping type federated search environment, the wide array of content available and processed in different periods under differing philosophies make that challenging to say the least. That being the case, while the institution may prefer to house the content locally to provide uniform access in addition to long-term preservation, the need for patrons to use different vendor platforms and search interfaces to locate content may not deter them from purchasing or leasing content from multiple different vendors with different access methods. In other words, the need for specific content to fulfill curricular or research needs may force larger academic libraries to compromise in terms of uniform access.

For the smaller institution, or public library, however, the need for one uniform user interface may be the overriding factor in licensing content. Use of one uniform, commercial interface also usually eliminates the need for the library to host the content locally, which is particularly helpful for those libraries without robust technical support. Many of the commercially available packages also include assistance with marketing the content to patrons, and have eye-catching web sites including cover art and other niceties not always readily available when hosting content locally. School libraries have slightly different needs as well, with a growing emphasis on the ability to correlate content with state teaching standards, to pick and choose truly multimedia resources from one vendor package to suit classroom needs, and the ability to integrate the content into other online resource packages such as aggregator databases. While the current digital environment is not yet equipped to meet all these various needs, there is at least a growing understanding between video librarians and the providers of educational content in particular that such options need to be addressed, and that there is no one-size-fits-all digital model that will work across all types of libraries and institutions.

CHAPTER

6

VIDEO ACQUISITIONS INTO THE FUTURE

Though video formats and specific processes continue to change rapidly and evolve in order to keep up with changes in the home market and current technologies, many of the underlying issues have remained constant for many years. There are, however, a number of potential changes in the video environment that may significantly change the way video is used in the classroom, libraries, and society at large. Some of these changes may affect all library resources, not just video formats in particular.

USER-CREATED CONTENT

The growing emphasis on the importance of user-created content creates challenges in making that content accessible to patrons in a timely manner and in preserving that content for later research or general use. Web sites such as YouTube (http://www.youtube.com/), Hulu (http://www.hulu.com/), Amazon Video On Demand (http://www.amazon.com/videoondemand), Mogulus.com (http://www.mogulus.com/), Stickam.com (http://stickam.com/), and Jumpcut.com (http://jumpcut.com/), which offer a variety of commercial and user-created content downloads, online viewing, or file sharing options are already being used at some institutions as alternatives to traditional library services such as physical format video reserves.

Purchasing or including user-created content in library catalogs is a very different proposition than purchasing or leasing commercially available content. The current environment is much more likely to place the burden for storage and retrieval of this type of content on the end user or the third-party provider than to emphasize the library's role in preserving and providing access to such content. If the trend towards quality user-created content continues, however, libraries will need to develop appropriate policies and infrastructures to provide ready access to such content as broadly as possible. Such plans may include working much more closely with content creators, with less contact with vendors and distributors, unless vendors also radically change their models to work with a wider array of resources. The difficulty for video producers, of course, is that they cannot currently compete with the abundance of free content available in a cost-effective way, so they can only rely on quality and reputation to remain competitive. Should the market of user-created content expand sufficiently in quality and reputability, the current vendor models will need to adapt significantly to remain viable.

Other upcoming changes in video acquisitions may most closely resemble how serial acquisitions evolved into the current heavily electronic environment. It is to be hoped that updated technology will continue to improve the quality of streamed and downloadable video, creating a viewing experience closer to that of the original release. While many film enthusiasts abhor the trend, as more content is created digitally there is less of a divide between the online viewing experience and the original format. While there is no end to the physical video format in sight just yet, particularly given concerns regarding copyright and feature film releases, it is conceivable that not too many years down the road much video content will be only available as a digital file rather than a physical format.

STANDARDS

One of the biggest challenges with many of the foreseeable changes in media librarianship is the creation of industry standards regarding file formats and licensing. Whether considering user-created or commercially available content, video librarians need to advocate for standardized file formats and licensing agreements that support inter-library loan or file sharing, and use of video within course reserves, in order to keep video content on a par with the rest of the carefully selected library resources made available to patrons. Too much content currently accessible to individuals online is not available to libraries due to restrictions in the licensing, which limits use to one particular user or computer. Such content needs to be promoted and made accessible in a variety of ways in order for libraries to continue to have a vital role to play in the careful selection and stewardship of content for coming generations, not to mention the ability of patrons to find quality resources to meet their needs in an otherwise overwhelming digital environment. Given our current understanding of the video marketplace and the needs of our users, perhaps the best future we can currently envision and work toward is one where acquisition of video content closely mirrors the acquisition of electronic journal content and can be made widely accessible to patrons with an eye towards long-term accessibility.

APPENDIX

A

Review and Selection Tools

The following recommended review, selection, and reference tools are taken in part from an earlier publication by the author, and updated with current information and additional new resources.[32]

Selection and Reference Tools

Bowker's Complete Video Directory

Published in four volumes annually, *Bowker's Complete Video Directory* is one of the more complete video directories on the market. Two of the volumes are dedicated to entertainment videos currently available for home distribution and two of the volumes are dedicated to educational and special-interest titles. The volumes are formatted identically, with ordering information and a short synopsis available in the alphabetical title index, while volumes 2 and 4 have additional cross-referencing indexes. Additional indexes include (but are not limited to) an awards index, a genre index, a cast/director index, a manufacturer index, and a subject index of over 500 categories. For libraries interested in only entertainment titles, or exclusively educational and special interest, the set can be broken up into two sets and purchased independently. The major drawback of this title is that it is fairly pricey, and, as with all video selection aids due to the nature of the market, must be purchased annually in order to stay reasonably up-to-date.

Video Source Book

Gale's *Video Source Book* is another fairly comprehensive guide to the titles available on the market. The *Video Source Book* is published annually in two volumes, the first edition was published in 1979. Unlike *Bowker's Complete*

Video Directory, the *Video Source Book* does not separate entertainment titles from educational and special interest titles. Instead, all video titles are included in the video program listings section by title. In addition to the program listings section, the *Video Source Book* includes six other indexes: alternate title, subject, credits, awards, special formats (including closed-captioned), and program distributors. The *Video Source Book* has coverage for more than 130,000 program listings, including over 160,000 videos. The *Video Source Book* is part of the VideoHound reference guides to movies and entertainment. A subset of the *Video Source Book*, roughly 25,000 of the movie and entertainment titles, is published as the *VideoHound's Golden Movie Retriever* guide, which is a great public reference tool. Also available is *Magill's Cinema Annual*, which is geared towards serious film research and provides essay reviews for the "significant" films released each year. Neither of these two smaller titles are anywhere near as comprehensive as the *Video Source Book* however, and are better used as public reference tools than selection aids. Like *Bowker's Complete Video Directory*, the *Video Source Book* is fairly pricey, especially for smaller libraries. Unfortunately, accurate and comprehensive coverage is best guaranteed by the purchase of both titles on a yearly basis, and even then there are some things that fall through the cracks.

Video Review Sources

Video Librarian

Video Librarian, published bimonthly, is one of the best video review sources around. The reviews are written by a variety of folk including librarians, teachers, and film critics in addition to the *Video Librarian* staff, and are geared towards public, school, academic and special libraries. There are roughly 200 reviews per issue, as well as feature articles on items of interest including new technologies. Reviews are divided up by major subject areas such as Children's, Education, Language, Health & Fitness and The Arts and there are separate listings for video movies and a DVD spotlight. Reviewed material is current, new to the market within the previous two or three months in its current format. Each review includes appropriate ordering information and data on the availability of public performance rights and other special features. The *Video Librarian* is also now available online as *Video Librarian Plus!* (http://www.videolibrarian.com/), which adds online access in addition to the print subscription. The online access offers a searchable database of over 12,000 full-text video reviews and roughly 1,000 video distributors. *Video Librarian* is one of the more affordable review resources around and is highly recommended for libraries of all types with a video collection.

Educational Media Reviews Online

Educational Media Reviews Online (http://libweb.lib.buffalo.edu/emro/search.html) is another excellent source of reviews for educational and documentary titles. The reviews are written by librarians and faculty in institutions throughout the United States and Canada. *Educational Media Reviews Online* uses a three-tiered rating system; all material is given a rating of recommended, highly recommended, or not recommended. The primary intended audience of the database is academic librarians, but there is a fair amount of material included that is appropriate for school and public librarians as well. Originally the *AV Review Database*, part of *MC Journal: The Journal of Academic Media Librarianship*, *Educational Media Reviews* came into existence in its current form after *MC Journal* ceased publication in early 2002. The database is searchable by title, subject, reviewer, year, rating, distributor and format. There are currently close to 4,000 reviews accessible through the database, and the cost (free!) makes *Educational Media Reviews Online* a very attractive review source.

Movie Review Query Engine

If you are looking for reviews of feature film titles, a fast, easy and free resource is the *Movie Review Query Engine* (www.mrqe.com). A note to keep in mind is that these reviews are not written for or by librarians for selection. Unlike other sources mentioned, the *Movie Review Query Engine* compiles reviews from various news and web sources such as the *New York Times*, *Chicago Sun-Times*, Reel.com, and many others. This can prove very helpful though, particularly if a patron mentions a particular review in support of a title purchase.

Other Video Information Sources

Cinema Sites

Cinema Sites (www.cinema-sites.com/) is a nice starting point for becoming familiar with the wide array of video and cinema content available online. An aggregator web site, *Cinema Sites* does a great job organizing hundreds of video-related web pages by categories such as Reviews, Previews, Movie Screenings, Films for Sale on Video, Movie Scripts, Film Schools, and Movie Enthusiasts' Pages to name a few.

DocuSeek Film & Video Finder

The *DocuSeek Film & Video Finder* (*www.docuseek.com/*) is an online database comprised of the catalogs of eight major documentary distributors (Bullfrog Films, California Newsreel, Direct Cinema Limited, Fanlight Productions, Icarus Films, Frameline, New Day Films and Women Make Movies). The database can be searched in number of ways, and includes grade level, length, awards, and other characteristics not typically searchable in other databases.

Internet Movie Database

The *Internet Movie Database* (www.imdb.com) provides a wealth of information about films, television, actors, industry news, and much more. The site is free online, and is searchable in a variety of ways including actor bios, plots, quotes, and specific TV episodes, which can be highly useful in tracking down hard-to-find content or incomplete citations.

OCLC WorldCat

Online Computer Library Center (OCLC), Inc.'s *WorldCat* is one of the best online reference sources for video materials. Introduced in 1971 as a union catalog for 54 college and university libraries in Ohio, *WorldCat* now houses over 125 million records from libraries around the world. This is by far the most comprehensive representation of video materials available, and each title is entered in MARC format, allowing searchability through all the major access points including Library of Congress subject headings. The drawback of the information being entered at the time of cataloging is that the distribution information, price, and availability are often out of date.

University of California, Berkeley Media Resources Center

A great online resource for information relating to a variety of video issues is the University of California, Berkely Media Resources Center web site (www.lib.berkeley.edu/MRC/). Of particular interest is the well-maintained list of Film and Video Distributors and Producers, which allows searching by name or partial name of distributor and browsable lists for documentary, educational, performance video distributors and producers, studio producers and distributors of theatrical and feature films, distributors and wholesalers of theatrical and feature films, and used or out-of-distribution video distributors. The site also maintains bibliographies on a number of film topics and genres and a compilation of resources for film studies.

Videolib and Videonews Electronic Discussion Lists

The American Library Association Video Round Table (VRT) supports two lists for active communication between media professionals. *Videolib* is designed as an open forum on a wide range of issues of interest to media librarians and other professionals including collection development, preservation, and copyright. *Videolib* also serves to connect video librarians with distributors and vendors. *Videonews* allows distributors and vendors to advertise new services and products. Subscription information for both lists can be found at http://www.lib.berkeley.edu/MRC/vrtlists.html.

Video Round Table Notable Videos for Adults

The Video Round Table of the American Library Association selects a number of titles each year considered to be the best releases of that year or the previous year in documentaries, educational and instructional titles, and performance works for adults. Established in 1998, the Notable Videos for Adults lists are intended to provide public and academic librarians with a core list of diverse titles which represent the best currently available on the market. The lists can be found on the ALA Video Round Table web site (www.ala.org/ala/mgrps/rts/vrt/initiatives/notablevideos/index.cfm).

Library Selection Resources

Video selection information can be also obtained from audiovisual sections in standard library selection resources. *Booklist* and *Library Journal* both include a section of non-print reviews. A nice *Booklist* feature is that every January there is a Booklist Editors' Choice list published which include video broken up into Video and DVD, Audio, and Audiobooks (also available at www.ala.org/booklist). *Library Journal* has separate video review and audio review sections in each issue. Though the quality of the reviews in both of these publications is high, the material being reviewed is often not nearly as current as those reviewed in the *Video Librarian*, and the selection of titles is much smaller.

APPENDIX

B

Glossary of Video Formats

There are numerous comprehensive, frequently updated video glossaries readily available online (see http://en.wikipedia.org/wiki/Video_formats for one example), so the intent of this glossary is only to offer a small sample of terms that may be helpful while reading this guide.

Analog Tape Formats

BetaMax. Often simply called "Beta tapes," the BetaMax format was a home video tape format developed in the 1970s in direct competition to VHS tapes. The BetaMax format is now obsolete, having been replaced by VHS tapes. Some larger video collections still have content on the BetaMax format and maintain playback equipment, though no longer commercially available.

Video home system (VHS). The most current of the popular videocassette formats, VHS tapes are considered by some to be obsolete, though many large collections are still viable, and dual-format DVD/VHS playback equipment is still commercially available. Similar to the U-Matic format, the VHS tape is a ½" magnetic tape housed within a cassette. The VHS format has been largely replaced by the standard DVD format, and most vendors have phased out production of the VHS tape, as the major Hollywood studios did by 2006.

VHS-NTSC (National Television Standards Committee). Tape format used predominantly in North America, Japan and Taiwan.

VHS-PAL (Phase Alternate Lines). Tape format used mainly in Australia, New Zealand, United Kingdom and Europe.

VHS-SECAM (Sequential Color Memory). Tape format developed by the French that can be found in France, parts of Greece, Eastern Europe, Russia, and Africa.

U-Matic. Videocassette tape (¾") recording format developed by Sony in the late 1960s, which was adopted as the industry standard for many years. One of the first to house videotape within a cassette, instead of the older reel-to-reel formats. Often referred to as simply "three-quarter."

Optical Disc Formats

Blu-ray disc. Named after the blue laser used to read/write these optical storage discs, the Blu-ray disc is essentially an upgrade to the DVD format with significantly higher storage capacity.

Digital versatile disc or digital video disc (DVD). Currently the most prevalent 4 ¾" optical disc in use for video and data storage. Replaced the VHS tape as the most popular home video media format.

High definition/density digital versatile disc (HD DVD). Developed by Toshiba as a potential replacement for DVD, the HD DVD is already obsolete, having been overcome in market share by the Blu-Ray disc.

Laserdisc. Now obsolete, the twelve-inch laserdisc was the first commercially produced optical disc for video storage. Though laserdiscs were never broadly adopted for home video, the underlying technology was the precursor to compact discs and DVDs.

APPENDIX

C

Annotated Short List of Video Vendors

Comprehensive lists of vendors and distributors can be found within the resources listed in appendix A, but this small, annotated list of useful vendors serves as a starting point for new media professionals who are not yet familiar with video acquisitions. It is intended to assist in particular with hard-to-find or out-of-print feature film titles.

alibris

A frequently used resource for out-of-print book titles, alibris has recently begun offering out-of-print video titles as well. Though the selection is still somewhat limited, the quality is high, and any assistance with out-of-print titles is extremely helpful. (www.alibris.com)

Amazon.com

Great as a basic source for many titles, and many out-of-print titles can be found through third-party vendors on Amazon, usually as used copies. Generally the third-party vendors offer legitimate copies, but there are often challenges getting such third-party vendors set up in acquisitions systems, particularly with many institutions tax-free status and limitations on the use of institutional credit cards. (www.amazon.com)

Distribution Video & Audio, Inc.

As noted on their web site, Distribution Video & Audio, Inc.,

> *[I]s an entertainment closeout company. Thus, we ask that you come to us with product that you are no longer interested in selling through your normal channels, or product that the license has or is about to*

> *expire. By doing this, we do not interfere with your sales or marketing efforts. We are not competition, nor do we want to be. Our mission is to provide you with a valuable service, buying your remainders and quietly make them go away to your satisfaction.*

As such, DV&A often has available titles that are no longer available through the original distributor. DV&A will search for out of distribution titles as well, with varied success. (www.distributionvideo.com)

ebay

Though many titles can be found on ebay, there are definite disadvantages to purchasing materials blindly through ebay. There is no quality check inherent in the system, and many bootlegged copies are billed as commercial releases. Unless there is a pressing need to provide access to a title not available elsewhere, extreme caution is recommended. There are also numerous challenges in purchasing materials from ebay through standard acquisitions processes. (www.ebay.com)

Facets

Facets extensive catalog of international film titles makes them an invaluable resource for many hard-to-find foreign films. Copy quality may vary a bit depending on the availability of a high-quality master, but in general a highly reliable vendor. (www.facets.org)

Midwest Tape

Midwest Tape is one of the few companies that provides ready access to single volumes of popular series, so is particularly useful when trying to replace one disc of the currently popular must-see TV series that will not stay on the shelves. (www.midwesttapes.com)

Movies Unlimited

Offers a huge catalog of titles and is a great mainstream vendor for most feature film and popular culture titles. The list of vendors and distributors of documentary and educational titles is immense, as the catalogs for most educational vendors tend to be much smaller in scope, in some cases limited to one or a few titles. Many high-quality educational vendors participate each year in the National Media Market (www.nmm.net), a professional conference for media professionals in academic, public, and school settings. The yearly list of exhibitors is an excellent starting point for becoming familiar with the big names and the smaller gems in educational video. The 2008 exhibitor listing can be found at http://www.nmm.net/market_2008eps .shtml. (www.moviesunlimited.com)

REFERENCE NOTES

1. Jean Thibodeaux Kreamer, "Video and Libraries: Present Status and Future Trends," *Acquisitions Librarian* 11 (1994): 19.
2. Audiovisual and Multimedia Section, "Guidelines for Audiovisual and Multimedia Materials in Libraries and other Institutions," International Federation of Library Associations and Institutions, http://www.ifla.org/VII/s35/pubs/avm-guidelines04.htm (accessed 23 July 2010).
3. Ibid.
4. James C. Scholtz, *Video Acquisitions and Cataloging: A Handbook* (Westport, Conn.: Greenwood Pr., 1995).
5. Mary S. Laskowski and Barbara J. Bergman, "Academic Media Center Collection Development and Circulation Policies: A Comparative Analysis," *College & University Media Review* 10, no. 2 (spring/summer 2004): 85–118.
6. Susan McAdam, "Selection/Acquisition of Non-Book Materials: Videos, CD-ROMs, Tapes, Etc.," *Acquisitions Librarian* 21 (1999): 145.
7. Scholtz, *Video Acquisitions and Cataloging*.
8. Joanne Salce, "Video Distribution: The Maze Made Manageable," *Library Journal* 115, no. 12 (July 1990): 42–44.
9. Ibid., 42.
10. Gary Handman, ed., *Video Collection Development in Multi-type Libraries* (Westport, Conn.: Greenwood Pr., 2002).
11. Diane Kachmar, "Acquiring Minds Want to Know: The Acquisitions Process of Videos and CD-ROMs," *MC Journal* 6, no. 2 (fall 1999).
12. Jeff Boucher, "COLUMN ONE; VHS era is winding down ; The last big supplier of the tapes is ditching the format, ending the long fade-out of a product that ushered in the home theater," *Los Angeles Times*, 2008, MAIN NEWS; Metro Desk; Part A, 1. http://www.latimes.com/entertainment/news/la-et-vhs-tapes22-2008dec22,0,5852342.story (accessed 23 July 2010).
13. Norman Oder, "The Format Dilemma," *Library Journal* (Nov. 15, 2002): 38–39.
14. Mary S. Laskowski and Chad Fennell, "Retooling Access to Academic Media Collections," *Technical Services Quarterly* 23, no. 3 (1996): 19–37.
15. Rebecca S. Albitz, "Establishing Access Policies for Emerging Media in Academic Libraries: The Video Lending Experience as a Model," *Collection Management* 25, no. 3 (2001): 1–9.

16. Ibid., 9.
17. Shiyali Ramamrita Ranganathan, *The Five Laws of Library Science* (London: Edward Goldston, 1931).
18. Michael Gorman, *Our Singular Strengths: Meditations for Librarians* (Chicago: ALA, 1998).
19. William Walters, "Video Media Acquisitions in a College Library," *Library Resources & Technical Services* 47, no. 4 (October 2003): 165.
20. Midwest Tape, http://www.midwesttapes.com (accessed 23 July 2010).
21. Gary Handman, "Searching for the Seldom Seen: Sources and Strategies for Acquiring Out-of-Distribution Videos," *Against the Grain* 15, no. 3 (June 2003): 42–46.
22. Alibris, http://www.alibris.com (accessed 23 July 2010).
23. Narda Tafuri, "Pushing Pause: Sources and Resources for Locating Out-of-Print/Out-of-Distribution Media," A Report of the ALCTS Out-of-Print Discussion Group. American Library Association Annual Conference, Atlanta, June 2002, *Technical Services Quarterly* 20, no. 4 (2003): 72–78.
24. Title 17, Section 110, http://www.copyright.gov/title17/92chap1.html#110 (accessed 23 July 2010).
25. Swank Motion Pictures, Inc., http://www.swank.com (accessed 23 July 2010).
26. Title 17, Section 108, http://www.copyright.gov/title17/92chap1.html#108 (accessed 23 July 2010).
27. Title 17, Section 107, http://www.copyright.gov/title17/92chap1.html#107 (accessed 23 July 2010).
28. Kastenmeier Guidelines, http://www.lib.berkeley.edu/MRC/Kastenmeier.html (accessed 23 July 2010).
29. Judith Thomas, "Digital Video, the Final Frontier," *NetConnect* (winter 2004): 8–10.
30. Sarbrinder Kaur and M. P. Satija, "Collection Development in Digital Environment: Trends and Problems" *SRELS Journal of Information Management* 44, no. 2 (June 2007) Paper L: 139–55.
31. Overdrive®, http://www.overdrive.com/default.asp (accessed 23 July 2010).
32. Mary S. Laskowski, "Stop the Technology, I Want to Get Off: Tips and Tricks for Media Selection and Acquisition," *Acquisitions Librarian* 16, nos. 31/32: 217–25; simultaneous publication in *Selecting Materials for Library Collections* (Binghamton, N.Y.: Haworth Pr., 2004), 217–25.

ABOUT THE AUTHOR

Mary S. Laskowski is Head of Information Processing and Management at the University of Illinois at Urbana-Champaign. From 1999 to 2006 she was Media and Reserve Librarian at the University of Illinois at Urbana-Champaign and from 1998 to 1999 she was Instructional Library Media Specialist for the Valders Area School District. She received a Master's of Library and Information Science from the University of Illinois at Urbana-Champaign in 1998 and a Bachelor of Arts, English from the University of Illinois at Urbana-Champaign in 1997.

Printed in the USA
CPSIA information can be obtained
at www.ICGtesting.com
JSHW020213210124
55355JS00002B/108

9 780838 985755